CONTEMPORARY
Macedonian
Poetry

*Selected and
Translated by*
Ewald Osers

KULTURA
FOREST BOOKS
London & Boston

Introduced by
George MacBeth

FOREST BOOKS/KULTURA

20 Forest View, Chingford, London E4 7AY, U.K.
61 Lincoln Road, Wayland, MA 01778, U.S.A.

Bul. JNA 68a, Skopje, Yugoslavia

FIRST PUBLISHED 1991

Typeset and printed by Kultura, Skopje

British Library Cataloguing in Publication Data:
Contemporary Macedonian Poetry
1. Macedonian poetry
I. Osers, Ewald
891.819108

ISBN 0 948259 67 1
ISBN 86 317 0068 1

Library of Congress Catalog Card Number:
91-70144

Contents

CONTEMPORARY
MACEDONIAN
POETRY

Introduction

One would like to confront every poem - from whatever part of the world it comes - entirely on its own terms, a bolt of melody striking for the heart. The art of music has encouraged us to feel for the common denominator, whether in an opera by Monteverdi or a piano sonata by Chopin. We listen to Wagner or Satie, however improbably, with a sense of standing on the same ground.

The illusion that we can escape the national accent has been fostered by the pop world, wherein the lingua franca of the American vernacular has created a shared body of reference above the familiar chords. But the limited resonance of those cast in the mould of Madonna explodes the myth. Even in the wider context of classical music, the international element is less frequent - and rather less important - than we might at first suppose.

All art - even the best of Titian or Shakespeare - is ultimately local: it must expect its deepest understanding from those who feel its roots in their own bones. A Spaniard is in the best position to enjoy Velasquez, just as a Scotsman is ideally placed to respond to Burns. Even allowing for the pressures of class and gender, of education and era, there is still an essential, and perhaps a pleasing, truth here.

One may embrace without guilt a nationalism whose manifestations are only cultural. There is surely something rather poignant in the notion of Wilfred Owen going to war in 1914 to fight for the English language.

But there is a difficulty here. While a cultivated person might reasonably be expected to know a little German and French, or English and Russian, or even Spanish and Italian, it will be a long time before many people can be found with a nodding acquaintance in both Arabic and Chinese, or Sanscrit and some of the African languages.

This means that the literature of non-European countries is often only available at second-hand to the English reader. A huge linguistic gulf yawns. Worse, this gulf is mirrored in the massive gap across which he has to approach even the literature of Europe, where this is composed in one of the less widely spoken languages, such as Finnish or Norwegian, Basque or Macedonian.

The role of the translator becomes a heroic one, even if it is that of a doomed hero. Without an adequate version in English, the best books of a whole nation will perish abroad, unable to survive in the air of a foreign country. So that someone like Ewald Osers, who takes on for the first time the literature of a part of the world most of us associate - and not very accurately - only with the name of a long-dead emperor, has a heavy burden to bear.

Macedonian was codified as recently as 1946, and the region it speaks for hosts the annual Struga Festival - one of the best poetry conferences in Europe. Two visits to this, in 1971 and 1989, have given me some idea of the keen appetite for poetry in Macedonia, as well as a notion of the fierce energy at work in the art. In allowing me the good fortune to be translated into Macedonian, these visits have also produced some understanding of the impregnable privacy of the language. I have seen supposedly accurate versions of my own poems from which I was unable to identify the originals, not finding enough handholds in roots or syntax to get a grip on.

Mr Osers has taken advice from writers whose judgement he trusts, and the result is a varied selection from about twenty-five poets. As he says, the problem was not so much in the selection of poets as in the selection of poems. There was no point in including a strong poem which was so full of local folklore and legend, or of references to Macedonian history, that it would have required an apparatus of notes.

The method of Mr Osers has been very much the subjective one of following his own nose - first selecting the poems he liked himself in the original, and then excluding those whose particular flavour would be impossible to convey in English. The result is a powerful anthology which may well take English readers by surprise, a switchback ride between poems of striking impact and originality and poems where a certain blurring of focus could impair interest.

Certain useful guidelines can be laid down. The reader may find these poems rather mercifully free from the too pressing domestic ironies of British verse. There is little in the vein of Larkin or Raine here, for good or ill. Macedonian poets have escaped from the prison of their suburban lives, though sometimes without retaining our own useful myopia of vision, at least in descriptive detail.

On the other hand, there is none of the clanking freedom we associate with some of the strongest post-war American verse. One would search in vain amongst these Macedonian poets for an echo of Ginsberg or C. K. Williams. There is little evidence that the deepbreathing lessons from the Black Mountain poets have been absorbed or assimilated.

The two streams of international poetry which seem to have contributed to this body of work are, perhaps predictably, the wry symbolism and wise-cracking allegory of some East European poets and, more unpredictably, the uncorrupted lyrical freshness and dynamism we find in the best Third World writers. There are moments when one might note a familiarity with the voice of a Pole such as Zbygniew Herbert or a Czech such as Miroslav Holub. There are other occasions when the poets seem to be aware of the passion and directness thrusting through in African poets, such as Christopher Okigbo or Atukwei Okai.

The mixture can be a heady one, and it should provide a stimulating cocktail for English readers. I won't dwell on the poems which fail to impress. Every anthology has a few of those, even Palgrave. More intriguing are the poets and poems that may stand out from the ruck.

Blaže Koneski, for example, born in 1921 in a village near Prilep, studied philosophy and has translated Heine and Shakespeare. His brief poem "The Word" offers the kind of spirited defence of itself which dimmer poems here could call on as an apology:

Regard the pointlessness of earthly springs,
whether of sulphur, or water, or gutteral shout.
This is an impulse poem, seek no meaning!

Elsewhere Koneski raids the medieval tradition in Macedonian literature and comes back with a coarse gem in "Sinful Women":

Oh the beautiful mothers-in-law
still unwithered,
those who, wide open,
have sinned with their sons-in-law...

There is meat for the western feminist here.

Mateja Matevski was born in Istanbul in 1929, and came to Yugoslavia with his parents shortly after his birth. One would like to sense a Turkish richness in his imagery, and perhaps there is a corolla of that around the penetrating intensity of his metaphor in "The Bullet":

when it discovers me and hides under my forehead
it will kill no more.

Few poems on the theme of racial identity have hit harder than this one.

But the major voice here, it strikes me, is that of Vlada Uroševiḱ, whose poetry has a wider range and more consistent sense of style than others, at least as Ewald Osers has been able to define it. Mr Uroševiḱ is the author of short stories as well as poetry and his verse bears the mark of a hard structure, which makes him a difficult poet to quote in detail; the whole poem is often what makes the point, not the individual images. There is welcome humour, too, in a poem like "Lack of Energy", which offers a satire on literary criticism.

But perhaps the most moving and original poem by Uroševiḱ, and one which offers a ripple of applications for the 1990s, is "Forbidden Zone", with its ending:

the guards are laughing.
We too are laughing,
even though we don't know what will happen next.

The perils of *glasnost* and *perestroyka* are implicit in these delicate lines.

Mile Nedelkoski, too, has something of the breadth and attack of Uroševiḱ. A slightly younger poet, he has written novels and screenplays as well as poetry. His "Terra Cognita" I take to be about the unworkable nature of Utopias ("I built you some little distance away from hell... How do I now demolish you again, you monster?") and his poem "Summer", by contrast, I read as a sensuous love-piece, where the season becomes the partner ("I pronounce you the most lascivious woman of the year.")

There are not many female poets here, but one worth watching is Liljana Dirjan, born in 1953 in Skopje. Her "Poetry Evening" offers a witty commentary on the aridity of a male-dominated literary criticism, which can fail, when assessing Emily Dickinson, to recognise the real woman in the presence of her bewitching techniques. The loss, Liljana Dirjan suggests, is its own.

I hope I've said enough to indicate the pleasure one reader - one writer - has derived from this anthology. As often before, Forest Books deserve credit for pioneering a field. Others may pick and choose where I have been blind, and perhaps one or two will even be moved to learn some Macedonian, and read these poets in their own language. Withering away through lack of need is, after all, perhaps the most glorious fate for an anthology of translation!

George MacBeth

Translator's Note

Every anthology - more especially one from a new and largely unresearched literature - inevitably reflects the translator's taste as well as his judgement on what elements of an unfamiliar background, what allusions to local custom and natural history, would be comprehensible and accessible to an English reader.

The present selection, featuring twenty-five Macedonian poets, is based on thirty-five volumes of poetry published in the course of the past twenty years.

I should like to gratefully acknowledge some help from Liliana Abbots.

Ewald Osers

Slavko

Janevski

Born 1920 in Skopje. Studied at the
College of Technology. Member of the
Macedonian Academy of Arts and
Sciences. Writes poetry, short stories
and novels: several volumes of each
genere. Has been translated into
Serbo-Croat, Slovene, Romanian,
Czech, Italian, Russian, English,
Hungarian, Albanian, Turkish,
German, French, Polish and
Esperanto. Winner of several prizes.

Pastel

There the hungry wolf
with his teeth
has ripped out the hot entrails.

There the fugitive convict
stone by stone
has dug his grave.

There the naked dead
on a table of their bones
have chopped up the moon.

There the rutting stags,
their antlers entangled,
have turned into skeletons.

There on hard arid ground
sorcerers have woven
a wedding feast banner from their veins.

The groom is the wind,
the bride is the mist.

Amazingly in their cradle
(a handful of earth and hope)
a nameless flower opens.

Let's go and name it:
let it be called *Dream*.

Looking for an answer

It left his skin on a stone
and turned into stone. A viper.

It grunted from rifle shots
and turned into mist. A wild boar.

It washed its eyes in foam
and turned into a sigh. Day.

In the village of Vraži Dol
Old father Time has sat down on a stone
and on his fingers
of wisdom
calculates
how many drops of blackberry wine are needed
to prolong his life.

You can ask yourself and still you won't know:
Does time die with man?

Markings

This race,
this wonderful race!

Here it kisses the hangman
with a golden noose round its neck;
here for a fistful of mulberries
it fights to the blood with a brother;
here it gets drunk with rage,
foaming at the mouth,
here it plucks the live heart
from a dove.

This race,
this wonderful race!

In its furrows
under the sun awakens
a flower with a biblical name:
Mother-of-God's-heart.

Breakfast with death

He doesn't come the way you thought
from rose-coloured glaciers
with a dead stag in his arms.

Quietly he creeps out of
the sunflowers' sparks,
his eyes are golden,
his hands those of a ploughman.

We meet like friends
on an ant's trail:
Death with a primrose in his teeth,
you with a cake under your arm.

The primrose of salamader skin
the cake of sweat and sand.

He with primrose wine
you with a mouthful of cake,
both in the jaws of time.

As you lay down together
on a bed of nettles
Death's nine larks
began a lullaby.

And the warm breezes too
fell asleep under the stone.

Threesome dance

Let's go and dance a little,
Death, you and me.

He'll dig a well,
you, with the well's bucket
will haul up my blood.

Death will sow tranquillity,
you'll water the tranquillity,
I'll harvest the bones for you.

I'll gather them into a heap,
I'll knit them together,
and while I still have one
I'll lock up my heart in them.

Death will take a ruby from it,
place the ruby in your hands,
you will strike my head with it.

Death above the stone,
you on the stone,
I under the stone;
you and he before the altar,
I a wedding guest in finery
underneath the altar.

When we've danced our fill
we'll part again.
Each by his own mill
to be ground down tomorrow.

Brotherly share-out

We're left without field,
our candle's buring low,
we share what we have.

You drink my eye,
for three eyes two hands are too much;
I snatch your hand,
for three hands two feet are too much;
you pull off my foot,
for three feet I take two ribs,
for two ribs I give two shoulder-blades.

You've shared out everything
you've not come to the end,
something's still left to you.
You, me, that,
I, you, this,
we'll share out everything to the last piece.

On the boundary
between two voids
a flower springs from the arid soil,
the one they called
two brothers' blood.
from Death's hands
the future still drinks echoes:
Brother, where are you?

Introduction to alchemy

You search for yourself in your mine,
you dig out your head,
it doesn't recognize you.

You put your hands in water
the left has gripped a grass-snake,
the right has suckled a mole.

Nether the one nor the other
has embraced you.

You'll find the feet,
which selfishly pass you by
and forget you.

Alone and without yourself
you'll ascend to Uranus
and, covered with your shadow,
you'll dream you belong to yesterday.

The foundrymen beneath you
will try to cast you
from ash and raspberries.

In vain.
You're not even in your poem.

Only that stone
with your name under the rain
will stay in its place.

Before the curtain falls

Only a little
only a little longer
than your sigh
the violin string vibrated.

Until then you didn't know
that Death heard that chord
under the crystal
for you alone.

I have no time to envy you
the moon lay down under my arm,
with crumbs from it
I feed the black swan.

I am sorry
you didn't have time to tell me
about the twin woodmen
who fell asleep on the magic acorn
or about the miller's son
who rode off on a lightbeam
to the magical fields of oats.

I don't know how to do that.

Blaže

Koneski

Born 1921 in a village near Prilep. Studied philology at Skopje University and worked there as a professor. Was the first President of the Macedonian Academy of Arts and Sciences. Corresponding Member of the Yugoslav Academy of Arts and Sciences, as well as of the Serbian and Slovene Academies, and Honorary Doctor of the Universities of Chicago and Cracow. Writes poetry, short stories and essays, as well as scholarly works, many of them on the Macedonian language. Editor of the Dictionary of the Macedonian Language. Translator of Heine and Shakespeare. His work has been translated into Serbo-Croat, Slovene, Albanian, Turkish, Hungarian, French, Russian, Italian, Greek, Polish, Romanian, German and English. Winner of numerous prizes, including the Golden Wreath of the Struga Poetry Evenings.

Among the trees

You've stopped as if buried in the ground and rigid
as if you'd sunk roots deep down
to grow,
seek moisture.

It would be better that you did not move -
that your hearing ceased in the rustle of countless leaves
which give space and shade to the birds
that sing,
better that you concurred with the wind
on one delightful symphony -
but best of all that you take no step,
lest you disturb the covenant with all these trees.

Skopje

You who will stand on Gazibaba,
you, my descendant hear me:
From here I too have gazed on Skopje,
it was a spring day, one of those
when the fresh outlines of the roofs
are softly interwoven
and every poplar is a green waterjet.
My gaze a little veiled
(that's why I'm silent)
but clear-sighted and bright.
Know you:
I feel that this my call
is the boldest grasp for the future,
an embrace of your soul, I'd say,
and cutting like a fresh-honed edge,
dreaming, teeming, screaming:
remember me!

The word

I've always reflected on the needlessness of the word
and that it least touches those to whom it is directed -
whence, then, this need to say so much,
what's more with rhythm, rhyme, alliteration?
Regard the pointlessness of earthly springs,
whether of sulphur, or water, or gutteral shout.

This is an impulse poem, seek no meaning!

The call

This voice of the muezzin
from a tape,
this velvet baritone
from the mosque,
this morning it sounds so persuasive,
like a link between earth and heaven,
so consoling and so calming,
and so deep at first sight,
that intimate contact!
And yet, if you understand the prayer's words
you'd realize that this is just a call,
effective only for the faithful
on this poor earth of ours.

Recollection after many years

I was perhaps not quite twenty
when I wrote:
"So much did woe cry out within me
that I was born into a tribe in need."
And to this day
the injury will bleed:
I'm haunted by that ever-present woe
and one that's greater still,
so that, sower of barren seed,
I'll say,
to change the words a little,
"Still does the woe cry out within me
that I am born into a tribe in need."

And yet I hope this isn't so,
since I have undergone the test
of such great woe.

Sinful women

According to the 'Tikveš Collection' (15th cent.)

Oh the beautiful women of middle age!
Oh the beautiful mothers-in-law
still unwithered,
those who, wide open,
have sinned with their sons-in-law -
there's no entry to heaven for them,
not through the strait, not through the wider gate!
What use to them are all the good deeds
they performed from the goodness of their hearts -
they should be put to shame, and publicly,
because
down on earth
they didn't resist
the lust from which blossomed,
suddenly, sweetly,
and only once,
their wide-open
bodies!

Small things

All these trinkets,
toys,
trifles, souvenirs,
small mementoes of great moments,
small presents from great friends,
one day
they'll lose their magic attraction,
their small warm souls,
to turn into cold bits and pieces.
Maybe the elm which has begun to die
now similarly feels that it bears
a lot of withered branches.

Epistle

Without you, Tyre and Sidon,
life has existed here for thousands of years
and will continue.
We humans are like grass:
crushed, dried, withering, dying.
The land alone remains.
We humans are like ants:
squashed, destroyed, and again gathering in a pile.
From here, sometime, began the march to the Indus,
who could have foreseen that?
Along the Via Egnatia Cicero went into exile
in Salonika.
Near Drama
Caesar's ghost appeared to Brutus
in the tent
on the eve of the decisive battle.
And fifteen martyrs were consecrated at Tiveriopol.
Naum built a monastery
at the source of the White Lake.
This land also gave strength to King Marko.
And yet,
has it not suffered humiliation?
Everything is ordained -
we depart
but the land remains.

Wild geese

This cold morning before Epiphany
the heavenly piano rings out
with intermittent sounds.
Wild geese are flying past.
Flock after flock
like verse after verse
they record a song of alarm
in the sky.
But I don't understand these winged letters.
Only the cry is the same
as in childhood (over Nebregovo).

Aco

Šopov

Born 1923 in Štip, died 1982 in Skopje.
Poet, translator, academic. Edited
several literary periodicals, managed a
publishers house, was Chairman of the
Commision for Cultural Relations with
Abroad. Published over a dozen
volumes of poetry. Translated
Shakespeare, Corneille, Rostand,
Krylov, Krleža and others. Recipient of
several major literary prizes.

The birth of the world

Knot upon knot.
Stone upon stone.
A petrified forest
all frozen through.
Knot upon knot.
Stone upon stone,
both of us also stone.
Night smoulders.
The word separates from the dark.
Blue coal burns in its womb.
O you who exist because you don't exist,
you are rocking the sky,
you are spinning the earth.

O you who exist because you don't exist,
the earth reverberates under the paving stones.
Stunned by its deaths is the word
which bursts all skulls.
Knot upon knot.
Stone upon stone.
I dig my grave with my exile.
Open me up,
curse,
you fortress of stone,
let me burn in the coals of the word,
let me melt.

Before the flowering of the flamboyants

Last night the earth wept,
dry and cracked like an overbaked cake,
last night blew the desert winds
and swept the sand into the cracks.
Changing its clothes the sea spread out its blue shirts
and yet it failed to pacify the earth.
Only the sky remained calm and empty,
as if nothing were happening,
as if it did not see this havoc.

Last night the earth broke up.
But perhaps these were the thirsty beasts
which roamed among the woods and the savannahs,
dying by dried-up waterless springs.
But perhaps these were the trees twisting and splitting
and with their leaves licking the arid soil.
Only the sky was brutally peaceful and empty,
as if nobody needed any rain,
as if it did not see this havoc.

Last night the earth writhed.
But perhaps these were people waiting for rain
as one waits for a first-born
curled up in a lifeless womb.
Before sunrise everything tires and everything falls asleep
where people are found and trees and beasts.
Over the sea float only tatters of abandoned shirts.
And with the sunrise, like the earth's wounds bursting,
(red-blossoms and fires all over the town)
flowered the flamboyants.

Non-existence

I travelled a long time, a whole eternity,
from me into your non-existence.
I passed through fire, through ruins,
through fields of ashes.

Through heat, through drought, through darkness.
I fed on the bread of your beauty,
I drank of the throat of your song.

Don't look upon these dry black runnels
which rend my face -
they are a gift from the earth's face.
Don't look upon the unevenness of my shoulders -
they are a gift from the tired hills.

But look upon these hands -
two fires,
two rivers,
a dark waiting.
But look upon these palms -
two fields,
two barren fields,
a mute lament.

I travelled a long time, a whole eternity,
from me into your non-existence.

Gogo

Ivanovski

Born 1925 in Skopje. Worked for
Skopje Television. Several volumes of
poetry. Translates from Russian and
Serbo-Croat.

Rest

Lower the blind over the window
let's have semi-darkness,
close the door soundlessly,
keep quiet.
And don't tell me anything,
don't ask me anything,
let's have silence.

For one moment I want to imagine I am alone,
that I have reached some turning point
from eternity,
where time has stopped still,
where I don't know anyone,
where I have nothing to take from anyone...
Where everything is
just as it is.
Somewhere where the silence of impartiality
evens out wishes and desires.
And like some distant traveller
without destination
put down my baggage for a moment,
then lightly with my hand brush off
the drops collected on my forehead.
Lower the blind over the window,
Let me imagine in the semi-darkness
that I'm having a rest.

Roofs

I stand on the hill and look down at the roofs of the town
a sea of tiles has turned its colours to stone,
red, yellow, blackened tiles conceal
the workday town, submissive in its chains.

But here everything's different from the workday
                                        arrangement
and something different must be done by you here -
strange: people have sung so much in praise of the infinite
but invariably they've put up roofs over their heads.

Sadness and rain

The rain knows nothing about sadness,
it only swishes down monotonously
soaking the roofs, the pavements and the branches.
But when your eyes are moist,
when sadness speaks in them,
then, pressing our palms against the window,
we're in the habit of remarking
oh what a sad autumnal rain -
and for a long time stay glued to the window.

Srbo

Ivanovski

Born 1928 in Štip, writes poetry, short stories and novels. Works for Skopje Television. Several volumes of poetry, some of poetry for children. A selection of his poetry has appeared in Serbo-Croat. Winner of several literary prizes.

Mystery

The moment when the blood ripens in the fruit
and when the girls carry cool well water
in earthen jugs.

The river calms the colours of the afternoon
a whisper runs across the trout's path
and the water-lily closes.

And is there in this game a hint
of some wonderful conspiracy,
a secret glance, a sigh?

We're standing on the bank
tied to the reeds
with the golden thread of mystery.

Mateja

Matevski

Born 1929 in Istanbul into an immigrant family, who shortly after his birth moved to Yugoslavia. He is now a professor in the Faculty of Drama Studies at the University of Skopje. He is also a member of the Academy of Arts and Sciences in Macedonia and Principal of the Arts Department. Known internationally for his translations and his poetry he is the winner of numerous prestigious prizes including the Blaise Cendrars Prize presented at Yverdon in Switzerland.

The bullet

This bullet so carefully manufactured
from a lump of heavy ore
into a cruel grain
in some country
in some place
this bullet this wild beast
this dark messenger of death
which memorizes every letter of my name
traces my ancestors
hounds my shadow
this bullet which seeks me in the universe
which penetrates my sleep
which buries itself in my fear
without reason without asking without by-your-leave
a grain merely on its way
to its target
from the muzzle-flash
to the shattered skull
This bullet from an unknown hand
from an invisible eye
from an unperceived breath
that wants to take the breath from my body
when it discovers me and hides under my forehead
it will kill no more

The birth of tragedy

When Aristotle established the real state
of affairs
and determined the means of transforming clarity into
obscurity
and when laughter turn to rictus
and the wood into a sword
pain already existed
Because the hand had long been modelled as a hand
and the word as a word
to expel evil from the world
But evil was within
even in the most exacting rules
and the most inevitable actions
And Dionysus drunk with wine and sun
had long been dancing round phallus and sword
forcing the plucked vermin to sing
And thus the song was born
While women veiled themselves in black
while towers burned and ships were sunk
and horses crushed the fruits of the earth
and the heart transformed itself into a dry crane
and blood left the body
That had no special links with heroism
nor the grief of loneliness nor the tears of deserted hearts

Yet the old philosopher would even now invest
those butcheries with pretty rules
of the play
while the audience continues
to applaud death

Crimson, crimson, crimson.

Like a song carried off
into the blue sea
of mountains
the sunset
drowns...

From grass to shepherd's pipe
from flock to cloud
all luxuriant
inflamed

From breasts to song
from step to fountain
all phenomenal
and pampered

A flock enamoured of the shepherd's pipe
a bell lost in a song
an eye crazed over a peony

Crimson, crimson, crimson.

The island

Suddenly to find yourself surrounded by vast water
strange water
at night without harbour
A motionless body not even rocked
by the moon
Creator of hopeless silence
of quiet
a lonely island on a lonely planet
not even a voice can help
not even a shout ·
across a land without past
Solitary as at the world's creation
when you must start on your uncertain walk
that leads to yourself
Raise yourself raise yourself on your hindlegs
like the forest of the lost island
which waves to the vast deaf ocean
awakening it
for some new light that can't be seen
but heralds an as yet unknown sense
a new sense
Beyond the horizon of memory and intellect
beyond the despair
of this new existence

The lake

After many a year and many a dream
I again returned
to the lake
with the sweet waters
hidden in the hill's loins

The sun's diamond's
still cutting it

Not a stone in its depths
nor grass to obscure its throat
under the waves
nor the bird with its prey

I'm only an eye the eye of the sun
that ruffles its ancient
waters

Oh leave me by this lake
leave me there
by the bitter lake
dead

Return

You're coming to me and I sing
of your non-return

From azure heights
from deep shadows
with years
with suffering

Why are you hastening
with your dying
through slow living

The earth has long absorbed
my song
my curses

Deaf time is not awakened
even by love's howling

The heart has forgotten you
only the wrinkles on my face
remember you

On my face
on your rock-face

Gane

Todorovski

Born 1929 in Skopje. Studied philology at Skopje University and works there as a professor. Numerous volumes of poetry. Co-author of several anthologies. He has been translated into Czech, Albanian, English, Serbo-Croat, Romanian and Greek. He himself has translated over forty books, mainly from other Slav languages, but also from Albanian, English and German. Winner of several prizes.

Map of Macedonia

Would it be possible with such aloofness,
with two or three talkative lines and
with two or three conversational colours,
to splash on a canvas the idea of
one's native land?

Well yes, it would be possible!

Our destiny is framed
like something turned upside down,
doubled up in pain the horizons of hope,
crushed the visions labelled refuge,
truth spread out on the palm of the hand
and the pictorial perfection of no way out.

But all you see is a compass and a map
and many pencils scattered about it,
sharpened if not smoothed,
so they can prove themselves in a proud role:
looking at lines we look at grief,
we look at our history -

What we have framed here is not just a sigh
preserved in another colour -

That, too, would be possible; quite possible.

Blackberry

Blackberry, droplet of God
Red-black mystery of earth
Defender of summer
Surrounded by thorns

You are the fruit of ripe pleasure
A gift to all those who need you
You lend bliss to our day
Which was parched and dry
under the lid of midsummer heat

Where you are not: unequalled barrenness
Where you are: delight in existence
You hang there heavy with the sun's blood
You hang there with a thousand eyes of ruby pride
And those who pass you by
you regard with the bloodshot feral eyes
of dying summer

May he who grabs you scratch himself
May he feel pain who cannot ask politely
May he suffer who cannot understand
the unattainable mystery of your
unapproachable beauty

You prickly proud beauty of summer's generosity
Live on as a lasting warning
to all inexperienced wantons for beauty
that sweet delight and the stars
are only reached through thorns

The dove

Is the sky still the sky
without the dove's wings?

It flew here so suddenly
frightened and alarmed
chased by some hungry beak

Dear Lord
Such fear it carried
under its plumage

Its heart hammered like hail
On the thin roof it cooed
It clearly was upset

Dear Lord
Such upheaval
burning
under those wings
as it raised them

Was it that invisible wound
that we humans call fear?

I gave it all I could
to provide for one moment
tranquillity, shelter and food
and human breath and caress
and protection
I gave it all I could
to grasp that moment
like undelayable warmth

It picked up its strength and quietly flew off
out of the cage of my monotonous shelter
Because the sky wouldn't be the sky
without the dove's wings.

Parting

You're leaving and not looking back
the age-old fear of turning into stone
now germinates in you like pain
that something passes and you're left alone

You're leaving and you carry much
in that mute threat of yours
without a note, forgiveness, or farewell
cold marble, dry-eyed, no remorse

You're leaving hurriedly and without voice
and flapping like a startled bird:
you disappear beyond return and soon
become a shadow, neither seen nor heard

Biography

I was born
That is an absolute fact

I've lived some time
That's indisputable

Who needs me?
Everyone must know himself

Am I in someone's way?
Let him ignore me

It's much too undesirable
to be chosen as the enemy

This life is fiendish
But I'm a fact of it.

I'll die only to prove
that I have truly lived.

By the old bridge in Skopje

Highcliff Karpoš, you Macedonian cliff,
Highcliff, bloodstained unfinished word -
is this where you left your name?

The Vardar is mute, coming and going,
day and night through the centuries carrying something,
tumbling dirt and illusions and names
unworthy, half-stable, rootless
trunks, stumps, destinies, empires, greatness,
carrying everything, shattering everything, dragging every-
thing
without restraint, without greatness, without dignity.

The Vardar is silent, there is no gallows,
not even a plane-tree!
This century has changed a lot of things,
today they kill without ceremony,
without drums, judges, bemedalled hangmen,
today the bridges have no privileges
as participants in famous deaths.

I search for your name, here on this bridge.
The passers-by are silent, silent the stones.
The river is silent. And your grave's silent too.
The Vardar has hidden it somewhere under its current
to keep it safe for your children's children.

Nameless bridge, Highcliff Karpoš's grave,
if you are a bridge resist this injustice,
bring Karpoš back at that hour of destiny,
in chains before eternity.
Bring Karpoš back, let him declare himself eternal!
Two witnesses are sufficient before the law:
you are the first and the Vardar the other!

Ante

Popovski

Born 1931 in Lazaropole. Studied
medicine. Several state and political
functions. Numerous volumes of
poetry and winner of several literary
prizes. His work has been translated
into Serbo-Croat, Slovene, Italian,
Albanian, French, Russian and
English.

Peaks

In great excitement he glanced back
to make sure his companions were following him,
then on he climbed again,
with bleeding fingers hanging on to rockface,
roots and branches.

And when he'd reached the top
he told them to look down into the precipice,
and doing so they realized
that at this spot the moon and the stars
were closer than the earth.
"This far," he told them, "it was up to us,
higher than this
only the soul can rise!"

Futility

Words are not life, and therefore they are eternal.
Surely there must have been a serious reason
why among all the languages of the world
only the Gypsy language
has no word for "to have".

I make a note of that. But this is futile:
you can't write on your soul using a pen.

Treacherous letter

The table on the church's wall was laid
with bread, with fish, a beaker of wine. And there she sat,
a lonely saint - young and despairing.
For centuries she'd waited for the painter to come back,
and when she realized he'd left beyond all hope
she only touched his paintbrush hanging on the wall
and the noonday around her brought to life a red-haired
                                                    boy
with freckles on his face. She recognizes him, she looks at
                                                    him,
she takes his hand - and kisses him!
That was all her revenge for all those pangs of solitude.
Thus she impressed the seal of desperation
upon the soul of God,
thus did she write her treacherous letter...
Thus did she fashion her unfaithfulness.

Record

Borghes relates a record from the East, according to which
red roses used to bloom in India's deserts
and on their leaves was written in golden letters:
> There is no other god but Thee...

A record from the Arabian desert speaks
of fruit-trees on the banks of Tigris and Euphrates,
which instead of bearing fruit
> gave birth to birds...

In a record from Macedonia we read
of crickets which each had four pairs of wings,
and on one wing was written in Latin and Greek:
> Nothing is lies, here is the truth...

This morning I asked the monk:
> "Where's sister Ephemia?"
> "In prayer," he said,
> "she's on her knees before the Holy Virgin, asking her
> to suckle the sick goat-kid brought in from the pasture."

Black angel

This summer in Ohrid's Saint Sophia
a young black woman
stepped into the church.

The girl at first stood in the centre,
then leaned against the wall, looked up above her,
and moved no more:

the ground imperceptibly raised her up
and amidst that immaculate sanctity and peace
she raised her head above the saint on the wall,

folded her hands in prayer
and smiled. A black angel hidden between the lines
of the Song of Songs, and not descended yet.

Memory

Sunset came at that hour
just for the sake of the lonely old woman
in our street.

In the red glow her verandah gleamed
as she drew water from the pump in the yard,
as she stopped at each flower-pot on the verandah
to water her flowers,
to whisper some words to them,
and as she then lit a candle
and started to sing of so many summers.

And all by itself
as she was singing and rocking, the bell
of the nearby church began to ring out.

Now, precisely at sunset,
the cross on the bell-tower shone brightly
and a bird would fly up from the verandah

and settle on the cross.

Terrestrial astronomy

With rudders operated by stellar winds
we might soon navigate all through
the universe.

But when we return
the sun will long have turned to ashes
and the earth be charred,

and there'd be no one to welcome us home.
That's why we're staying here, tied to the earth,
having dug it up for centuries

and learned from the bones in it
that the whip moves faster than sound
and life faster than any light.

Psalm 2

Studying medical sciences I am
excited by the fact
that man has in his blood

exactly the amount of iron
that would be needed
to forge sufficient nails

for one crucifixion. I wonder:
who will unravel Sanskrit
while we are journeying to the stars?

Each one of us, I think, is some future Christ
because with his own blood he can sign
his disappearance.

When they separate the little lambs

When the cold mists and winds take over,
the shepherds dampen down their fires,
nail wooden shutters to their windows

and start to drive their herds down to the sea.

When spring erupts two stags come running past,
and then on chestnut horses come two shepherds,
they light big fires in the valley

and call out to the big stars in the sky.

After a week the flocks return,
the first night they lie down together, and next day,
at sunset they separate the ewes from their lambs.

A piteous wailing rises, moans,
and bleating of the innocents as the sky turns red
- as if the Christ child were torn from his Mother.

If you wished

If you wished, anything would happen:
this line would yield its place to another line,
the rivers would reverse their flow,
and cold would change to fire,
and past and future would exchange their places,
and people would grow young again
and would no longer think back,
and I once more would be just a step or two away from you,
and thus the normal state of things would be restored.

The shepherd's cross

Only one of the crosses in the graveyard bore no name.
A tendril with a few leaves had wound around it.
And underneath the shepherd sleeps his sleep,
who once, some distant evening, cradled in his arms,
brought us our first-born lamb.

That night in your bed

"That night in your bed
there were three of us: you, me, the moon..."
    Octavio Paz

Sometime on this plain, in this translucency,
when a fine house rises before us
with a bird flying through that air,
there'll be a window,
and at nightfall, as you come past,
a girl will open the window
to listen to you softly singing:

    That night
        in your bed
    there were three of us:
        you, me, the moon...

Jovan

Strezovski

Born 1931 in a village near Struga. Studied philology in Skopje. Since 1960 Director of the Struga Poetry Evenings. Several volumes of poetry, a few novels, and a large number of books for children, both poetry and prose. Some of his writings translated into Serbo-Croat and Romanian. Winner of several literary prizes.

Late flower

It blooms in autumn
Not having much time
it opens its coloured little capsules at once
sharing out its riches.

And while the wind works away with its saw,
making a coffin for it for the autumn,
it shares out all it has,
like a man his bequests before death.

Rare cactus

My grandfather brought me a rare cactus
from his pilgrimage
once a year it would blossom at midnight
briefly
and wilt
For a time before its flowering
we would wait for it daily
And the moment, you might say, was a feastday
There it flowered and wilted -
and my grand-dad would say excitedly:
To it it makes no difference,
but we sit watching it from hour to hour
to get a glimpse of transience

Pain

It comes unexpectedly
like a stray puff of wind
and cleanses you

While it is in you
it strengthens you
it rings in you
When it disappears
you're empty:
The stone has rolled down
but the place where it was still hurts

Passing through you
it pierces you like steel in angry water
tempering your spirit

Star trail

In the multitude of stars
flashes a shooting star
blossoming like a rare bloom
and dying

Was it impatient
did it grow in foul weather
or was it in a hurry to use
its turn for death

All eternity gathered it up
for a short trail

Icon lamp

From all blades of grass
it parts at night and recognizes them
by their gleam
Like a firefly that has landed

When it's quite ripe
Grandfather collects it for strength
for power

It's hung on a beam
for years
Its heart is dry
overdry

But at every rocking of the ceiling
it seems to us
that the gleam it has lost
is back again
flying all round us
Like the light from an extinguished star
that flies alone through the universe

Premonition

Sun and Moon have halted in their courses
They stand and look at one another
Luminous but not warming
The trees each have two shadows
without in any way shaping them
or giving them life
The nightingale as a messenger
flies off to announce some terrible news
but its voice is stifled

Into the heart's forecourt
winter creeps
From its wind
the soul trembles

Petre M.

Andreevski

Born 1934 in a village near Demir
Hisar. Works for Skopje Television.
Several volumes of poetry, several
novels, some plays, some children's
poetry. He has been translated into
Serbo-Croat, Romanian and other
languages. He translates from
Serbo-Croat. Winner of several
literary prizes.

Harvest

Two armies are facing each other
neither yields

Each soldier on one side
grips a crescent moon
the others have nothing
nowhere to flee

Yet there are so many of them
their shadows are blending

Above them the sun's bee-hive
sings hymns to the summer
(The earth burns skyward
fetch the well in your jugs)

Two armies are battling
the smaller one is victorious

Round shapes

(In praise of woman)

Round are your eyes
and the places from which you regard me,
directing my movements.

Round is your mouth
which taxes your words
and glorifies your smile.

Round are your shoulders
and round is your neck,
the only scaffolding from which
my whole native land is visible.

Round are your breasts,
those mobile bell-ringers
and guns raised in ambush.

Round are your nipples
and the honeycomb on them
and the milk mine,
first breeding ground,
first encounter with nourishment.

Round are your groins,
roundly they spread,
evenly they return.

Round is your waist
and the wind spinning round it
like a wheel on its axle,
like yarn on a spindle.

Round is your navel,
that scar of birth,
reminder of the spot
where life began.

Round are your hips
where light is rejected,
only entrances
into darkness and night.

Round are your knees
which I expect to speak to me
and round are your heels
which separate you from the ground.

Round is your embrace
when you kiss me, when I kiss you,
and round is your tear
when you part from me.

Round is the table
where you eat your meals,
and the bread and the plates
are as round as the table.

Round is the apple
you offer your guests
and round is the rainbow
in the water melon you cut open.

Round is the water
which you cup in your hands
and the water which parts for you
to let you bathe.

Round is the seed
which you sow in the field
and round is the downward path
by which its root descends.

Round is the sun and the sunflower
which rises for your sake,
for the sake of your roundness
without it I wouldn't know where to look.

Love letters

(from a cycle FIVE LOVE LETTERS)

I.

Nothing is more visible
and nothing is more present than your absence:
not the childish whispers which I discovered
in the crops of the rain,
nor the hint of storm in the cobwebs
in little roadside bars,
nor aerial paths lit up by swallows,
nor that which acquires shape only in my hearing,
nor my hearing while a belated cricket
winds up its nocturnal clock,
nor the birthpangs of the scattered seed,
nor the flaming fire on the cockerel's head
while it runs from the shade that descends from the sky,
nor the space which remains to me between your hands,
between your two hot suns,
nor the snake which ruffles the top of the corn,
nor the snowdrifts and hailstorms in poppy fields,
nor the flame which rises like autumn mist
in the fields of pepper,
nor the love and hatred between key and padlock,
nor the hidden light in a purchased match;
nothing is more visible than the trail you left
before me, behind me, with me and in me.

V.

And I sought you in textbooks, I sought you across the ages,
in the wind's ambushes, in winter's mortars,
in uncomprehended shame on the horizon before sunset,
in uncomprehended longing of a strand of tobacco
which twists and crumbles between the fingers,
in the displaced light of the blind and the dead,
in the equilibrium between past days and future nights,
in the captivity of souls of glass-blowers.

I sought you in the accents of unknown languages,
in the unsaddled evenings and empty beds in the field,
in the surprise primrose behind the herb-seller's ear,
in the punctuation in the speech of whining children.
I'm seeking you in the wild chance of unification
of my scattered nation,
in a stalk of sorrel, in the unused air
which annoyed and appeased the neighbouring villages,
by the anvils of hot and feminine afternoons,
among the fruit hastening towards its seasonal goal,
in the needle which sewed up darkness and light.
I sought you, listening for the underground drumbeat
that was the heart of sleeping harvesters.
I sought you beyond the sky, in heavenly molehills,
in the unread electric meter of an extinguished firefly,
in the assassination attempts by my people against my
people,
in the undistinguished constancy of the points of the
compass,
undistinguished, and understood as a constant waste of
time.
I sought you in the unfinished fear of the shooting star,
unable to reach anything in space.
I sought you, I'm seeking you in all and everything.
I sought you, and seeking you I might only have met you,
but not found you, no, not found you.

Vlada

Uroševiḱ

Born 1934 in Skopje. Studied literature at Skopje University and works there as Full Professor in the Department of General and Comparative Literature. Numerous volumes of poetry, short stories and literary criticism. Author of several anthologies. His work has been translated into Serbo-Croat, Slovene, French and Polish. He has translated over thirty titles from Macedonian into Serbo-Croat and some twenty from the other languages of Yugoslavia and from French into Macedonian. Winner of numerous prizes.

Lack of energy

The aged king -
elected for one more sun year -
feels his end drawing near.
The earth no longer brings forth millet,
the pumpkins by the river aren't as juicy as before
and the buffaloes are getting thinner and thinner.
His weakness passes to the land:
he knows it.
He has not visited his women's quarters for a long time.
He dozes and murmurs, he waits
to hear the heavy footsteps at his door,
dark whispering,
the extinction of his fire.
And so we sit by cold stoves,
in the middle of winter, without hot tea,
by mute television sets, in the dark,
unable to read Eliot,
let alone to talk about Frazer.

Cosmogony

Emptiness gave birth to the sea snail.
The sea snail to the volcanic island.
The volcanic island to the crested lizard.
The crested lizard to the Milker of the Clouds.
The Milker of the Clouds to the Honey Thief.
The Honey Thief to the Builder of Cities.
The Builder of Cities to the Tax Collector.
The Tax Collector to the Destroyer of Fortresses.
The Destroyer of Fortresses to twenty thousand tanks.
The twenty thousand tanks were barren
and couldn't give birth to anything.
And so once more emptiness settled in,
wondering if there was any point
in starting all over again from the beginning.

Drowned cities

Drowned cities -
that's what the midday rain reminds me of:
greyish blue, umbrellas, and beyond the window-panes
women sitting, a smudged photograph,
a little faded, with blurred edges:
tired girl typists, secretaries
looking severely from behind glasses, cashiers
absorbed in their sums;
absent for a moment, listening to
the rustle of the rain, but at once again
engrossed in their work. The rattle of
the typewriters makes the rain a little less audible.
But the rivers are swelling; some streets
can no longer be crossed. The drains are choked
and gurgle; the city
cannot absorb all the water that's pouring
down roofs, down walls, down those windows
behind which are seen their long legs,
their restless fingers. At one time
they'd opened the fountains, they mislaid the lid of the
                                        spring,
they helped the rush to burst through. Ondines, Melusines,
daughters of the torrent, avengers of the underworld, high
priestesses of springs in caverns, witches who
dance naked on river banks, conspirators who in the night
open the city gates
to let the sea in, traitors who against all rules
secretly entered the subterranean Sterna
and widened its opening, letting in the dark water
"that it may cover, that it may stifle, that it may drag,
that it may satisfy itself in the vastness", as the poet says.
Where are they now? The sound of the rain
can be heard in the offices where they are working:
they receive sheets of paper, answer the telephone, observe
an official attitude. Hello? No, he isn't here. Call again
a little later. The cities may be drowning, but these women
close up the crack in the wall with reports,

with files, folders, columns of figures,
and stamps. The men are yawning,
doing crossword puzzles, checking
their football pools. Nothing again,
they say; never any luck.

Distant sea

In Hesiod, among numerous wise pieces of advice
there is one that says: "As soon as on the top of the fig-tree
leaves appear
the size of a magpie's footprint, you can sail out on the sea".
Well, this is mid-April and on the fig-tree outside
the leaves already are like little magpies' tracks.
The trunk has already drawn up the sap from below;
gloom is turning into food. No,
I am not preparing to travel anywhere, yet suddenly
I catch myself thinking
of the rejuvenated sea in spring, muscular,
with the movements of an eel, eager to throw up spume,
mad and corrosive like milk
on unripe green figs.

Descent to the sea

The Slavs, driving down
to the south, towards Ulysses' fatherland,
encountering something that slumbered
blue like a magnet, stunning and frightening,
came across an old man who was carrying
an oar on his shoulder and asked him: Isn't this
a flail for grain? Tiresias
(for that's who he was) stopped;
although he understood
the talk of the birds, although
he had lived the life of a man and the life of a woman,
                                                    although
ha had lived seven times,
seven lives,
was confused. Blind, extending his hands in greeting,
he said: Traveller, are you returning again?
But those who had asked
were already far away, shouting,
like once the Ten Thousand:
"Thalassa! Thalassa!"
but in another language.

Fatal misunderstanding

This is some film.
This must be some film,
otherwise how could there be
so many red-headed women,
so many beautiful landscapes
and so much killing?
But what am I looking for inside
and how have I turned
from a spectator
into a person
who is being chased
and who
in the end
must
die?

Forbidden zone

We're going where it is forbidden to go.
Terrible punishments threaten us.
Though they aren't specified.
We creep through empty yards,
past abandoned building sites, then past houses
which only have façades
behind which stand household items
as if for decoration.
We cross the line.
Just then one of us stumbles,
making a lot of noise, raising
a huge hullaballoo
under the embankment.
Appearing
from the darkness in which they had lurked,
the guards are laughing.
We too are laughing,
even though we don't know what will happen next.

Mile

Nedelkoski

Born 1935 in Prilep. Works in the
Kultura publishing house. Several
volumes of poetry, several novels,
several screen and stage plays. His
work has been translated into
Serbo-Croat, Slovene, Romanian,
Hungarian, Italian, Turkish, Albanian
and Russian. Winner of three prizes.

New Year in Istanbul

For a moment I thought
I'd better decide where I am,
at first, with regard to this evening:
green and transparent
the sky, as if cleaned and buffed with floor polish
    after its daily pollution,
next, with regard to the city on the shore of the sea:
not allowing it either to dry up or to overflow
it perpetually ensures for it the same destiny -
turquoise blue visited mostly by birds, children and ships,
small motor boats
dark blue and like warts
on the face of the harbour.

Then I remember that I was alone at the fortress
    sitting on the ruins of the ancient basilica:
hymns, smell of incense and the burnt-down candles of time
on my lips and on my forehead drops of melted wax.

When I descended into the town again
I had to watch out not to lose my way
    or to fall into a ditch,
because the entire area was levelled and plunged into
                                darkness.

A certain tune came to my mind
    and I began to whistle it on the way,
thinking that it might be whistled just the same
by some guard on the ramparts of the city.

No other time had I ever been closer
than I was that night to your depraved heart,
Byzantium.

Archaeological motif

The great mosaic of the peacocks is being restored,
tar is being heated and drips hot
on bare feet, on the soul
standing above the body flung down on the grass.

Round the dead beetle of time
buzzes the white seed of the sun.

Terra cognita

I built you some little distance away from hell,
with an exit to the warm sea.
With one puff I raised up the mountains,
covered them with forest and allowed all kinds
of animals and reptiles to roam in them,
let fly all kinds of insects and birds,
raised up the sky above them, a home for myself,
and then I let all bitter and glorious waters free,
and rivers flowed, and streams, and in them fishes,
I appointed a ruler for you, a man of wisdom,
who from his palace balcony on feastdays
will wave a white handkerchief,
I also set up councillors, with healthy stomachs,
able to digest anything,
colonels who'll lose all crucial battles,
court ladies, courtesans, jesters and merchants -
all this I managed without much effort
one Saturday evening, when,
unable to fall asleep, I'd nothing else to do.
How do I now demolish you again, you monster?

Bridge on the Drim

1.

Who made the marble cry
but left no record of himself -
Over the water, in the air, fever seethes,
the bridge is in love with sighs of lapis.

You are my accidental quest.
I am not touching you, but you're aware
that once you're mine now,
you'll never be anyone else's.

When you are gone, a vacuum will stand
on this bridge here, a statue with your face.

2.

One word, flung from the bridge
into the goblet of your body,
falls like a silver coin -
I look through your transparent skin.

These fishes I've dreamt up
to keep a watch on you
are motionless and sad upon the shore.

With upraised hand, gentle, you're passing through them,
just as your love
now passes through
my time.

3.

Your breasts: two bells by whose sound
I remember the realm of your body:
fragrant of sour cherries,
where my own country lies.

Your breasts: two bells with whose sound
I wakened the realm of your body:
I conquered it, even though you yourself
defended it; I spied on it.

4.

The water's body
and your body's shadow on it
in the base of my eye.

The sun's milk is dripping on the bridge.

Summer

I pronounce you the most beautiful fruit of the year.

My lover
gives birth in the hay-rick
to the bastard conceived in the barn.

I pronounce you the greatest sin of the year.

Propping up my tortured body on the dry air,
I come to talk about
harvest and wine and your sun-tanned legs,
between my palms I squeeze southern death.

My little bastard girds it with a curse
and sends it off on the wind.
Who can now convince me there is wind in the field?
With the red drop of poppy it doesn't look like a Turk.

I pronounce you the greatest wanderer of the year.

I arrive in July and the familiar mushroom
spreads its hot smell.
Behind the crest of my eyes marriages emerge,
great as grief.
In my blood thirst is begotten.

I pronounce you the most lascivious woman of the year.

Song

In darkened and secret rooms to be christened, naked.
The conjunction between your blood and mine will tie up a
preposition
and fire and water and wind will not be in time to conclude
it

I repeat: I appoint you ruler and doorkeeper
of these heated seedbeds of naked bodies
and I've opened the door to you.

Petar T. Boškovski

Born 1936 in a village near Kruševo. Works for Skopje Radio, mainly on cultural, scientific, educational and documentary programmes. Several volumes of poetry. Co-author of anthologies. Has been translated into Serbo-Croat and Albanian. He translates from Serbo-Croat. Winner of several prizes.

Butterflies

Lightly they descend on the landscape,
the colourful butterflies of spring,
like tremulous sighs,
like blossom from heaven.

Innocently they settle on the greenery
which last year the merciless caterpillars
stripped down to sadness so it should give them
the wings for this year's beauty.

But now it gives you the right to flee
fiercely as if seized by madness,
and let no one ask
what's happened to your good sense.

Fresco

On the left sidewall of the church in Glušino,
painted with talent and skill,
you'll see a small area left as a riddle:
a patch of bare plaster big enough for one more saint.

It's not that they didn't know what to do with that spot
or that there wasn't any money left for that small patch,
or that a quarrel had arisen about the orthodoxy of the
painting.
It must be a sign of some blind misadventure:
it was struck by a gang of bandits and cut-throats,
swamped by an army of unbelievers and dragged away,
struck by cholera or mown down by the plague...
It was something that kills the god in man,
but was not recorded by our impoverished ancestors.

The little church remained as it was then.
One might say that this isn't the work of a human hand,
that this spot of a slap in the face was not a place
where, thinking of its master craftsman, you should think
of a man.

Spring in the forest

Something aroused me from a dream
and I went
to see my own eyes

As I bent over
a wild forest grew up
from them, touching the sun

Then I was seized by a fast current
of gentle falling,
demanding only my soul

From the topmost and softest air
I separated the purest water
and kissed its brow

Yet I don't know where it began
to tempt me into madness,
the silver restlessness of an undiscovered legend

But the first yellow leaf of the old forest
dropped to the ground before my eyes,
sending me back

Since then
that silver restlessness
has remained in my heart

And in my blood
ceaselessly teams
that undiscovered legend

And I no longer dream of the spring in the forest.

Iris

There is a place
where the wild iris reigns

Nowhere before have I seen
so many deep blue flowers
paths full of liquid fragrance

Are they eternal wounds
caused by the strike
of rain's blue flame

Or only tenderest consolations
for hard agreements
between bodies and earth?

There's one warm period when
the mournful iris reigns

The unsatisfied souls of the dead
seek healing in its buds
yet remain unhealed

From one deserted grave
an old grass-snake loyally serves the flowers,
its legacy is called silence

I saw that place but once
or else just dreamt about it
unafraid I turned back

That place exists
where the sick iris reigns.

Nocturnal fantasy

Who has so diabolically painted
the lyricism of the wind
under the branches of that lonely plum-tree

The wall wants to be a canvas
for the caressed trembling of the leaves
of the golden palette framed by the window

Whom do I have to thank
for this view which has become a sigh

The young plum-tree heavy with fruit
and through the garden a warm wind
which comes in gentle waves

From the branches to the wall
the moon spins powerful strings
for the night's guitar with fragrance in the sounds

Come teach me to speak magic to you,
meek element, gilded dance

The fruits are swelling with the moon
dropping to the ground with delicate skin
the wind is fragrant with late summer

That picture tied to things and occasions
dawns from one end of the night
such beauty in a room is bound to be stolen

I'll stay to guard you while you're here,
insomnia is singing in my blood and eyes.

Summer romance

They spread it out beside the baskets,
the underwear, too, because it got wet -
how did they let that happen?

They'd gone up the hill to pick raspberries
and the river tempted them -
what would they say in the village if they knew?

The sand with inflamed eyes
danced over their bodies,
stirring sweet passion

An old man coming from the woods
looks at them, shakes his head:
they look to him like creatures from a story

In this ticklish going-on
do they have a (handsome) young man in mind -
what would they say in the village if they knew?

And here refracted in the water
three nudes of young girls
whom the pool was painting in a trance

But the pool, the devil take it,
unleashes amorous cries
Yet has weak hands

The white garments are drying,
summer drops to its knees
trembling with passion

What would happen if they knew in the village?

Black river at Mariovo

People have come
to meet the oldest remains
that exist of the face of the earth
some power robbed them of the way back home

They didn't expect you
but when they found you it was too late:
desires had become
too distant to see

Oh Black River
why did you make
this long deep canyon
so you now have
only a narrow belt of sky in the water

As for the birds you catch,
you blacken their wings
and hide them spread under boulders

Unable to return
to their pastures,
a huge herd of ancient fauna
remained turned into stone from feebleness
bloated from too much water in their stomachs

One stream strikes
the golden wire
and turns in a circle from madness
which no one will recognize

On your banks
where during the day
a thicket was
gurgles the black water

Refusing obedience
to your flow
people are engrossed in argument with fishes

Your are not pleased about the hurricanes
there's nothing for you to feed on
but no one says the land is worthless

Ah, water which is here,
no one should have you,
here you received your black name.

Mihail

Rendžov

Born 1936 in Štip. Studied law. On the
staff of the National and University
Library in Skopje. Numerous volumes
of poetry. He has been translated into
Serbo-Croat and Romanian. Winner
of several prizes.

I was returning home

I was returning home
by a road of excavations and gravel piles
And returning with me were
my Little Things:
the pebble with which someone hit me long ago
the drop of blood from my nose
the fruit I stole at night
the forest where
a bird hid from me
(after some forgotten poem)
the sins I committed
defending myself
the angel I forgot
while quarrelling with friends
the life I let slip by
staring at god knows what
and god knows where.

one night
all my Little Things
were at home
only I was not there

I am lost, they say,
staring at god knows what
and god knows where.

Morning poem

Wash your eyes,
open them to the sun
and leave your peacock to puff himself
just as my mirror puffs itself up
when you negligently
pass in front of it.

It is time I told you
that you're a beautiful Letter
with which each morning
I begin my poem:
the illuminated initial
of longing.

Auto-da-fé

I am on fire.
Red-hot.
Burning.

I am counting the constituent drops:
one drop: birth
one drop: passion
one drop: wonderment
one drop: fear

What the last drop is
I don't know
Probably the drop: nothingness
Something like a possible remnant
of life.

We walk holding hands

We walk
holding hands:
Angel and mountain
Nightingale and silence
Soul and darkness

We walk holding hands

We walk
holding hearts
Wild beast and mountain
Sparrow-hawk and silence
Worm and darkness

We walk
holding hearts.

Windows

When they built the monastery
the master craftsmen made the window glass

translucent.

Through it
entered pain
and a little light
from eyes full
of tears.

At last,
when the eyes had wept themselves dry
a swarm of fireflies and stars
settled in the monastery
and burst all over

the vaulting.

When it is snowing

When it is snowing
it's like the sky trying
to bury my sadness

The stags climb to the ridge,
not from snow
but from sorrow

all white

They fall, softly they fall

They fall, soundlessly they fall,
the drops of the night

Heavenwards grows a flower
shaped from dark crystals

They beat the air,
soundlessly
opaque words beat

the silence.

25 January 1981, Nerezi

The entry into Jerusalem

(A fresco)

We stand here: He all bright
I dark. Suddenly
the waters opened up -
the sanctuary doors closed.

From the soul then
rose nightingales
and vanished behind the walls.

Does it mean I have entered into Jerusalem?

No, I have not entered;
they have brought me out from there.

Nerezi, October 79

The deposition from the Cross

(A fresco)

When they took Him down
they wept.

The Cross seemed like a bird;
From His wounds myrtle flowed
on to His face, ah, that face,
yellow fruit between two rows of stars.
Angels came flying down to Him,
white basil flowered for Him.

Angels came flying down to me,
white basil flowered
on my face, ah, my face,
yellow fruit between two rows of stars.
The Cross seemed like a bird to me;
From my wounds myrtle was flowing

When they raised me up,
ah, when they raised me up

they wept.

Nerezi, August 1976

Ascension

They made a rope
and thought to themselves:
The noose will soon choke him
and he will fall
as from a deadly wind

Then we shall entice
jackals and eagles
to peck out his shadow
make his dust disappear

But behold: a miracle.
The noose turned into a halo
and He did not fall
Here He

ascended.

Nerezi monastery

Forgotten expanses
of green and blue
Forgotten games and miracles
Forgotten flashes
of brightness and darkness
Forgotten soft blankets
Forgotten the lake of the sky
Forgotten the lake's bottom

Forgotten colours and trowel
Forgotten angel craftsmen
Forgotten towers and balconies
Forgotten bells and palaces
Forgotten flutes and drums
Forgotten brides and hyacinths
Forgotten time
its silent march

Illumined
Overarched.

Radovan

Pavlovski

Born 1937 in Niš. Numerous volumes of poetry. His work has been translated into Serbo-Croat, Slovene, Albanian, Turkish, Hungarian, Romanian, French and English. Winner of several prizes.

Corn field with crows

(From a cycle of poems entitled 'Van Gogh's Summer')

Out of the light, hidden, they fly in,
a flock of black crows. They peck one another,
pluck one another, croak and twist into a storm
over the corn field. They want to take something
from me and from the ripe corn
and to shade me under the Starry Roof
of Summer, and I, thus darkened with a colour
that was unexpectedly born, fling them
on the canvas and store the ripe corn
in a barn from a Star.

The sun at Arles

(From the same cycle)

I harness the Sun
but it both resists and seduces
like a young bride at first kiss
on her wedding night. Between countries and peoples
shouldn't there be tenderness, home, mother or lover?
I want to multiply or not to be, I don't know which.
Whenever I sing or love I'm always fettered
like a demon for that Sun and for that Now

I'm tortured both by Desert and by Fruitfulness

Under the precise and high blue sea
a white chalk line and the shadow of a cloud
of unearthly rain - mysterious
blue-green hieroglyphs of Ra,
his ashes yellow, without dew,
perpetual garment that will also be food
for my sunflower

Scattered the seed of my sun
in the furrows of the world
And what can be done here now?

Two deities -
one in the sky, the other on earth,
like twins they are in constant touch.

Instruction

When I die
carry me
on a bier of metaphors

Don't put me down
from the shores of one sea
on to the shores of another
Leave me to rest
Let the distant weep

When I die
don't close my eyes
continue your love
with blind insignificance

When I die
don't carry me dead to the River.
In the world's eye
bury me.

Gypsies

Dispersed like dark drops of rain
in the heat,
they have neither church nor prayer,
nor realm to wage war.
For others they forged a sword,
for themselves they sang a lonely song
And him who sang most beautifully among them
they chose for their ruler.

Orpheus looking back

He turned to Her and She revived.
She's fallen asleep over my song.
Did she want me to stay in love
and unborn? Prophecies
came from light
like the combined voice of cockerels.
Was it the snowdrop nurtured by the snows,
as I within myself counted the waves?
I searched for you.
I roamed.
I roamed.

No.
There is no death.
Heaven is innocent.

Bogomil
Ǵuzel

Born 1939 in Čačak. Drama director of the Skopje Playhouse. Several volumes of poetry, stories, plays and essays. Co-author of an anthology of contemporary American poetry. Selections of his poetry have appeared in Serbo-Croat and English translation. He translates from English. Winner of several prizes.

Nostalgia

Grow, grow up
my son - eucalyptus

Grow for me, grow,
dear eucalyptus

in other climes
under foreign skies

where the sun warms
as it does here

Poems

In the beginning was Darkness
and here it is now, at the end

In between there
was Light here and there

and many sparks dancing:
one me, the other you, etc.

only flashes in the mind
and then nothing

        * * *

Since there's been flying into Space
the bird built its nest
in its own shadow

The Sun, setting,
fell into the hole
dug for it

by agents of Darkness.

Vita nova

Death comes to us like a chimney-sweep
with sooty face and bloodshot eyes

to burn our old lives
it burnt itself and burnt the house down

and the chimney collapsed
(the rain then washed the house:

pay for a job only half completed)
How shall we live without a chimney

with an open fire
beneath the cold stars?

With the fire between us
from which we burn

we won't even be able
to see each other

and there won't even be a woman chimney-sweep
to collect our ash

Envoi

1.

The world is changing my poem
but my poem's also changing the world
at least my world

My world is the poem
My poem is the world

And I -
a mask over emptiness?
Whose -
spirit or matter?

I am in my world and in my poem
I am what alone need not endure
but without which both poem and world can come to a
full stop.

2.

What will be seen first
is who and what is

Something? Nothing?
So much the better

But at least I was
Upon me fell a ray
of primeval light

And then it went away
when I let it.

Off you go, I say to it

3.

I'm coming, it says

Ridiculous worry

You can't be "too much i' the sun" (Hamlet)
however much you may wish it

because you're placed under the protection
of a parasol

and if you dare to close it
you will be stifled by its protective wings

Delphic oracle

This body is the lyre of Apollo
and you are plucking its strings
Perhaps you'll extract a sound not heard before

perhaps at last you'll shoot your arrow
into the quarry that so far each time
has managed to escape

Delphi, 1.5.1980

Eftim

Kletnikov

Born 1946 in the village of Negrevo. Studied Yugoslav literature and Slavonic languages. Works as a journalist. Several volumes of poetry. Co-author of two anthologies. Has been translated into Serbo-Croat. He translates from Serbo-Croat and Russian. Winner of several prizes.

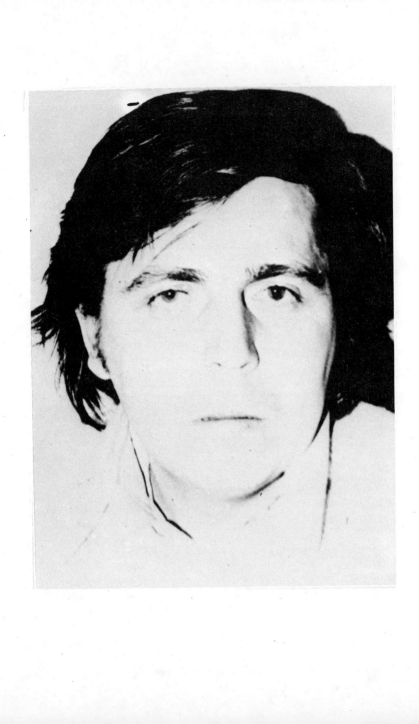

A jug of mountain water

(Note from Lazaropole)

You fell asleep so fast
as if the mountain had
covered you up.
Suddenly - in your dream a crash.
The jug has shattered,
fragments of earthenware are flying round,
the water spills, gurgles
and grips you by the throat;
the watery face of the forest spirit
is growing.

Alone, you scream
and instantly wake up.
The door of your room is open,
the jug stands in the corner,
in its usual place,
full of water.

You only listen;
somewhere in the forest
bubbles a spring, and the water spirit
is happy again to have escaped
your dark earthenware jug.

The shepherd

The sky's blue waterfall is rushing
as though the quick mind of the shepherd
had burst into song
as overhead, grown heavy from the cheerful weather,
a flock of birds tumbles about -
God's thought,
which sends out wing over his hut and pail,
and then, fast as a dart, is gone
through the herd's udders
which start to fill with milk.

Is this the moment when God thinks of milk,
or are the sky, the sheep, the shepherd and his pipe,
the spring, the star and blood
just milk?

Lie down beneath the udder
as under the central cupola of the church.
Listen to the harebells ringing
like the angel's golden wing
and watch the dark-grey stones
get overgrown into a fleece.
From all these mournful places
God drives his milking herd
out to the pasture.

Even the apple defends itself

Don't think
the apple is powerless
when you spy
its gentle rosiness in the branches.

Maybe this is only a sign
that it is warning you
while you are being seduced
by its weakness.
Therefore don't dismiss
its threat.

Let your lips this moment
disregard its
intense sweetness.
For can you be sure
that its pips do not harbour
the winged spirit of the fruit
(firebird with root-wings)
or that in revenge
it will not sink roots
in your pillow
so you never
wake up again
from it?

The young man's crimson scream

They found the axe.
Then they dug deeper.
They discovered the town where
the sun is forever at sunset
and the square is blood-red.

They also discovered a crimson scream
which by day flies like a nestling
but at night turns into a young man
with a rounded kiss
blossoming under the shore of the girls.

And we have heavy dreams:
groans of the executioner and the axe
where we have dug,
and in the morning, still not fully awake,
we catch sight in the mirror
over our shoulders
of the head of the young man
from whose lips flew the frightened
bird of his crimson scream.

Song of the Negrovo church bell

Less and less do they
ring out
less and less do I hear them
as I move further from childhood.

But I remember that ringing
was not in vain.
Each sound was a golden grain
that dropped on my dream-field.

Something now makes me
gather the harvest
grown heavy and overripe,
because it's getting cold.
I'm beginning to write
this song of the church bell.
And at each turn an Angel
brings me bread and wine.

Waiting

And the door was open.
And the window too.
We were waiting.
Hearts and rafters
broken with pain.

Where did you lose your way,
why didn't you come, God?

You didn't endure the night,
you extinguished our little flame.
And we were so frightened for it.

What if afterwards the sun rises,
huge and indifferent -
like yourself, God.

You forget the dead

You forget the dead,
but one day they will appear
with the riches they left
to increase: with goats and sheep,
with pails and with milk,
with grain and with barns...

That will come to pass
when terrible hunger and thirst arise,
when the springs dry up
and the water-mills stop turning,
when through the empty rooms
of your house and heart
only hatred and cold will breathe.

And only with them will there be
love and fire,
bread and a glass of wine,
sustaining you, never empty.
They - sensible and rich,
you - unreasonable and greedy.
Insatiable, and then
you will upset their glasses
and foul their dinner table.

But they, in revenge, will withdraw altogether
and leave your dream to yawn
with emptiness forever.
But their house will be brimful
and yours empty.
You'll go out to hunt,
but you'll shoot nothing but the pine-cones
of your despair,
which, wounded already, will roar through the disconsolate
                                                woods
of your angry heart.

Sande

Stojčevski

Born 1948 at Studena Bara. Studied
literature in Skopje. Works for Skopje
Radio. Several volumes of poetry.
Author and co-author of anthologies.
Translates from Serbo-Croat. Winner
of a literary prize.

Snowdrift

A sledge of strong desire
and heavy snow all around,
deep in thought
as when you are late for an important date.
Wafted over by drowsiness
an exhausted deer suddenly jumps
and from the wooded silence
a wolf-pack of hatred emerges.
Past the fire, dreamily,
a blizzard flashes
stuffing the signs, all frozen
and crumpled, into its pockets.
The rickety window, expectation,
and our glances, with foreheads pressed
against the glass, caught a cold and coughed.

Sound

Among the pine-trees and the mist
suddenly war, and we are all alone,
small wooded patches on a big hill.
You're hiding butterflies in your thoughts
and, like gold coins in a narrow cave,
breathlessly you cover them up.
In your unattained south, on the cherry-tree,
ripen your fears.
For a long time I hid you in dense sounds,
your doubts I sent off drifting in a boat,
kept safe in canvas like ancient manuscripts.

Moon

Before the high tide, before oblivion,
we met our sisters,
restless, grass-eyed, night-haired.
We wanted to dance a little,
to play hide-and-seek
excitedly urged on.

And deep defiles,
propriety and maturity,
open before us.

Part of an entry

With a premonition we arrived
at her wide gates.
We stopped for a moment
as though no one was there.
We forgot ourselves
on our voyage to the eternal fire
as though we were holding
cold ashes
in dry hands.

Over the most fragile branch
we carefully tend
shadow and hope
because we are returning from a dream.

Smoke

September in the valley
and furtively the branches
come down to the very fingers.

Distant and rather cold
your thought advances
to snow-capped hills,
where you can just about be seen
extinguishing the forgotten candle
in a ceremony
that scarcely endures.

Undesirable

I was ready to sail off
on a large chunk of air,
to become a permanent resident
of cheerful oakwoods,
now and again to swing
above the world
like an unborn year,
to be the wind,
transgressing the line
and crumpling the carbon paper.

But too many undesirables
have I chosen for enemies.

Atanas

Vangelov

Born 1946 in Bogdanci. Studied in Skopje, now Professor of Modern Croatian Literature at Skopje University. Several volumes of poetry and literary criticism. Winner of two prizes. A selection of his poetry has been published in Serbo-Croat. He has compiled an anthology of Macedonian poetry, published in Albanian.

Blue snowdrop

I brought warm violets,
gentle greenery,
I brought a pearl of water.

I mixed them with silence,
from silence I gleaned
big bright smiles.

I planted them in the deep sky:
the smile in the sky
smelled sweet and grew leaves.

When I was not working on it
my work spoke of me, gave proof of me -

the blue shout of the violet,
of the water, of the greenery
growing paler...

You watch the flight, delightedly,
the flight eastwards emboldens you
because you are there.

And yet, you don't understand: your delight
springs from quiet uncomplaining death,
from the blue snowdrop

which is extinguished in the snow.

Corn and light

Against the light the corn ripens

and there's no silence that can mark more clearly
the kinship and the painful intimacy
that divides them.

He who gave himself to it, continually,
who breathed in its young face,
who multiplied its speech
brightened by darkness, heavy,
darkened by a tall earth -
he must understand that
against the light the corn ripens.

Dear parents: your distant brightness,
so secure, outstrips me.
From the corn's stony husk
I read your absent faces
when the time approaches
for full kinship,
for bursting.

Again the darkness will elucidate for us
the cloudy gleam of intimacy,
then the remorseful breathing of the earth
will bring the future back to us,
and then, far from the stars,
from ourselves,
we shall meet again in falling.

Light falls over the corn
like my mother's gentle glances
over my harsh, my bitter words.
And brightened words,
painful with brightness,
are ripening
against the light.

Falling

For Kiril Paunovski

We were striding fast:
maybe we felt that
the intimate space
was crumbling and small,
the space made by night -
that soon it would burst
under the blow of the heavy,
merciless sun which
we could hear already.

There were no roses.
Scattered in the air
they yet piled up within us.

In no way do we understand
muteness and loneliness,
such nocturnal blindness -
necessary for agreement,
for intimacy for everything
that happened between us.

Oh unheard-of roses,
midnight warm roses:
we passed and we drowned,
we drowned as we passed

under deep rivers
of perfumes,
under soundless rivers
and as far as we understood -

there was a falling,
not painful but bright
and even joyful.

Vele

Smilevski

Born 1949 in a village near Demir Hisar. Studied philology in Skopje. Works at the Literature Institute of the Philosophical Faculty in Skopje. Several volumes of poetry and essays. Co-author of a five-volume publication on Macedonian literary criticism. Selections of his poetry have been published in Serbo-Croat and Albanian translations. Winner of several prizes.

Hitting the target

Open flesh
sheltered from wind.

Red curtains over the threshold.
One more step
(since the night passed in a gallop)
to the target
which pops up
as I aim at it.

And you say:
The core has a deeper meaning
and the journey there
doesn't wait
from this sheltered spot
from this unbuttoned room
from this store of overripe seed
life
begins.

You take her breath away

You take her breath away

inside
deep
she is soft

to the extreme

to the point of madness
circles the bird
in the window

eyes
transformed into wings

to the extreme
inside
deep

soft
to the point of madness
is your bed.

Breakfast

We exchanged our dreams
and everyone now silently
is stealing the rest of wakefulness
from the mutilated night.
My morning happy pill: vitamin A

Blessed is the bread
and the emptiness filling it
like parted lips
before our
insatiability.

Platefuls of sea
and the aquarium of the sea
roar from the sea's depth
The word which only now
will be ours alone.

The door

It yawns and chews it,
all that emptiness
which perhaps tomorrow
will harden
into words

And yet blank sheets
and papers fly
I clutch a few words in my hand
to squeeze them out
and dry them for gunpowder.

Easy therefore with the lighter
for, lighting my cigarette,
I flare up like a wick
and blazing, appalled but without shouting,
I'll cross the threshold.

The bird

I drew a bird I drew
the fragrant wind too
so the pencil's lead
could resist
      be a
      cage
and hear what's unspoken
in the poem

Meanwhile
dense ozone
has open our pores
and the mortar rang out
rhythmically on the wall
and the marble sang
while I was descending
to a blank sheet

And under the whiteness
in the base of the lead
the bird was flying up into the poem
and the cloud under the lightning
carried an egg-shaped quartz

Restoration

Here was the eye
there the hand.

It's raining from the cupola
some sky invites us
       to fly.

The foundation is groaning and trembling
some earth invites us
       to dig.

Here was a man
in short a lover
our age, dull-witted under the chisel
and invisible under the brush
which obliterates me.

Katica
Ḱulavkova

Born 1951 in Titov Veles. Studied
literature in Skopje; works at the
Literature Institute of the
Philosophical Faculty in Skopje.
Several volumes of poetry and some
literary criticism. Has been translated
into Serbo-Croat. She translates from
Serbo-Croat and French. Winner of
two prizes.

The mysteriousness of your tongue

The tongue is never sufficient unto itself

The hymens of words are bursting
spattering blood - an unlyrical saliva
penetration lubricated in sagacity.

Fragrant lances sink inside
but right inside
the tongue's anagram is
an insatiable game
from my gullet to yours

The more archaic
the more festive
the dialect of love
the hymn of the lips
the red forecourt of the throat

give it to me
spirally
spiritually
ritually
honey-baked
peasant bread, tongue-bread
tongue on the spit, earth rust-red
take it from me
give it to me!

We think up lingual digressions
excursions to pure regions of the world
reciprocal situation plays:

The god of our tongue is dead
(therefore he's God)
now we have every right
to reshape him
to change him
between us, so that magnanimously
we're consumed by fire

both in dream
and in reality.

The neck

- a neuralgic spot -
    The neck - a gateway to Mycenae
    (not all the tombs are open to the public)
    from the dregs of the subconscious - history
    there turns its objects of value
    forward and backward
    art not for art's sake
    the twentieth century arrives unexpectedly

    The general bewilderment is not enough
    to change woman's appearance
    the provocation of her neck
            "In certain conditions
            the archetype is detrimental to..." or
            "The cult is organic matter: it is not lost
            - it is transformed", etc.

news that makes us happy:
youthfulness of appearance (Modigliani)
vines of a new kind of beauty
- and Tsvetayeva's invisible fingers
on the back of a long stubborn winter
a mime of silent protest

all in all
the anti-grammar of despair
- know thyself

moreover (by association from the neck)
straits which pulsate - hope squeezed tight
a gorge in which a double bass groans
and manly argonauts
from other worlds
do not abandon their pursuit
the entry into woman is infinitely long

your will be done
your free will!

The common place

Oh how warm it is
oh how moist it is
your soft-boiled
blood-sprinkled
eye-catching
blackness
   I'm thunder
   she's wonder
Oh how steep it is
your wooded
suck-loving dexterous
your cosmic
shepherd's staff
your burnt
yet burning leech
your thick lip
an order, your
hungry year

I uncover the picturesque
open-work of pasture
I fill the aquarium
with a watery world and excitement
I draw both aloud and from memory
every letter is the first letter
in the alphabet of phallusophy

aleph

Time for your medicine

You to whom it's not all one
readers
leaders
it's time for your medicine
water, willingness
for you to say Still
though they didn't know
that love survives
as Ludwig did the war
    nature and interior settings
    are stage directions
    music and rain
    elucidate the king's nature

I'll now move off
and you try to be different
get your umbrellas and handkerchiefs
your sense of direction, for an early walk,
your sense of flooding,
and you who get wet, who've come alive,
come closer to the fire
so you don't catch cold
don't turn your back on it
nor your face,
moving along
form a circle now,
perhaps the metaphor will be simplified
let someone command you
"fold your umbrellas, it's cleared up"

but you can still feel
the drops
can't you?

Menace

Understand me
I can no longer
create you
heal you
with postage stamps
you shall no longer
roam about
I wish
to believe

The moths
are eating
the addresses
within me
Intimately
some icebergs
are melting
and bitterly
the shadow
of time
is falling
when vines
and urges
are pruned
but the plant
flourishes
luxuriantly
like sin

Open your mouth

When you abandon yourself
headlong
turn your back
slam the door
you grow
you flood
call into question
the height of the banks

to explain that
you're talking about the soul
you open your mouth
sigh
- yet love overpowers you
face to face

when you leave yourself
suddenly
you take your blood, honey
unsolved questions from childhood

What is man?
Your step gets heavier all the time
as you cross the frontiers
you know yourself that you aren't quite yourself

You exhibit doubt
at all events
the soul has its facets
which you cannot abuse
which you cannot betray
so you cannot return
so he cannot return

but nothing can beautify the feet,
fructify them, believe it or not,
show your hands what a deluge is
and make a report

if they don't understand you
open your mouth
blow!

Open sea

For sailing I took with me
soft cloths in different colours
to wipe the salt
off and from under my
dried-up, cracked, water-hungry skin;

and binoculars, for I have always enjoyed
watching phenomena capriciously
their visage and size
vanishing before my eyes
unnaturally deep or shallow
with a right to choice;

and paper, for the blood I spit
for taking notes prematurely
about the dance of fish and roe
an anthropomorphous dance
for corresponding with ideologies
on which I set my seal
as on someone else's experience
forgotten property

or perhaps
for divining what lies ahead, agreeably
but never faithfully to my intention
my hope-for-hope's-sake;

and a dream, to assemble
longings and climates as non-identical
as people
to look at images and wake up
to turn into images
        because not even yours, sea,
        is sufficient for me
        to understand myself
        to come out into the open.

Miloš

Lindro

Born 1952 in a village near Ohrid.
Studied science in Skopje. Published
several volumes of poetry. Translates
from Serbo-Croat and Romanian.

Lost meaning

When I pass through this life again
for a second time, when
the world's ends change sides
and the sky grows enormous, a steep field,
its crystal fruits
with brightness to your taste
and the lost meaning of sin
with a wonderful turn to that
step
    towards infinity
      towards that non-sojourn,
from suspended rays of a warm touch
we'll flee to diamantine distances
into the recesses of empty suns
and into spaces quietly carrying
the greying echoes of our dream.

One special view

Just look around you
take a good look
this is about something special
something constant but special
something we don't have time
even to notice
something that perhaps
doesn't want to be noticed
something indifferent
something omnipresent
something outside everything
something beyond the intellect
something ironical
from which one returns
(like small visitors from outer space)
something soundless
which produces a breath
and sometimes silence
as fear exists under the sky
everyone seeks it differently
but we all agree
that it is GREEN
and without any
connection with death

(because that itself is
the connection and unnecessary)

Doubly two-faced

The circle which, while it doubts, shouts:
Help, please, help - damnation is here;
and then: Still, still, still I am the same;
his damnation, his deep loneliness,
his property, the indifferent world,
this entire song - his song of lamentation
becomes deception, becomes a trick, becomes a bluff,
a borrowed voice, a stolen yoke, a violent gesture,
deliberately sad, calculatedly perfect,
even though, after all, somehow, objective
whenever, o Lord, it is miraculous and seen by us.

Escape

Let's get into the words,
into foreign words
because we don't have our own,
because even ownership
is just a word,
a word remote and mute
which cannot either have
or possess itself,
the word the cheeky appearance
which reaches out to cubic words,
some of them deaf and faceless
but pleasant enough to look at
with a clear conscience beyond the threat
before which one retreats;
maybe safety represents us
but escape is necessary
until ability becomes
one terrifying occupation:
the cause will be lost,
the objective will rock,
but ability will remain
unstoppable to the end.

Warning

Too much talk in the dark, too much
head-shaking, provoking
such boldness, uncalculated,
while the victorious gurgling incessantly
reminds us, like an ancient lesson,
of behaviour in solitude, in battles
with trifling blameless possibilities
(Countless firelike drops -
heavenly water for the thirsting)
They remained quite unshakable,
zero-clean and sturdy followers
in the face of demonic whispers,
in the face of divine silences.

Semitic song

A beduin night of which one doesn't know
if it has fixed suns or not. A broken
camel's leg beats time for the horizon
to gleam in longing in onyx in sweet fragrance
The thirsty animals are our neighbours when the wind
stops rustling the stars that have fallen by the banks.
Over there to the north is the tomb of Ishmael
and the meagre blood from the mountains
dreams the same step every eternal day.
Along dry wadis and dead seas
Lot's dead daughter drags herself
with golden clank, from dark skin
flows darkness, neither whispering nor promising.
Above them a splendour of confused dreams
evenly sinuous warm movements
vanishing in blue looks.
The same sand in death and ashes;
the same silence in battle; voice and desert.
When we thought our longing was true
the child prophets came and proclaimed
the coming of ETERNAL BIRTHS.

Liljana

Dirjan

Born 1953 in Skopje. Works for a
woman's magazine. Some volumes of
poetry. Winner of two prizes.

Poetry evening

We sat among Emily Dickinson's 1775 poems
(that, at least, was Thomas Johnson's approximate sum)
those two knew English and seized upon finesses
they were passing a pencil to each other to mark
                    the powerful passages
They talked about internal rhymes
untranslatable structures
complimented each other on their skill and precision
every so often jumped up from their seats
and returned to the text again

Between them, like a second, I waited:
which would draw his gun to kill me?
Poor Emily
could never have expected
that her poems would be some use
that they would kiss in the air...
While I crumpled up
the target grew
and they fired like poetic experts
accurately
without noticing in their excitement
how I unbuttoned my life
and faded away.

Hello, Orwell

1984
Across polar winters and nights
despair arrives
I welcome it with gifts
The flat smells of the pinewoods in my dream
I wash its face with snow
I lay the table for a welcome feast
me and him
amidst the shining plates and the glasses of water
we call our friends from a past poem
to renew the cause of revolution
"Be a revolutionary", "Be an anarchist"
Let's get out of quotation marks into the fresh air
me and him
into the fresh air
to sup on darkness, to drink blackness
to tell each other openly who stands for what
but when we've worked our way through the real words
I'll put my head into the fiery oven
and he'll describe the situation
and disappear

30.12.1983

My mother dreamt I would no longer write poetry

I will not be a civil service clerk
I have one more moment
dramatically to fall into your arms
while the tundras renew themselves
and the Caucasian snow chokes our
ancestors up in the sky
you bleed medievally
I see you prone in the river bed
flowing through yourself
and your children are learning
lessons from the darkness
perhaps with some other reality
I touch your face
to determine your depth
and already in the mirror
my face shrinks and wrinkles
and before it even takes its shirt off

it shivers with the cold at the end of the 20th century

When I move in

When I move in
there's an unfamiliar naked warmth I have
100 inhabited and 160 desert
islands under my eye And
I'm falling like
unrepeatable rain over Fiji
(on Fiji it rains 180 days in the year)
180 days to the hour
my love
moisture
which destroys our walls
and moulds spawn
I said to you: I've come
but you, still behind the looking glass,
are learning to walk,
gently, somehow.

Salt mines

Not only because of the absence
of a landscape with human figures and
a plate with cigarette stubs and
dialogue
food matter
plus
home-made bread
but
because it defines me
in the kitchen
among the packets of produce
in bed
a refuge of love
equally
with water and dry land
a duality
she in the bread and the sea
I from her and the sea
has become thirsty
has become heavy
and repeated itself

For lack of evidence

The oyster
(oh, my wide-open eye)
is an island of bone and marine content
proximity, change, seen and touched
slurped up and come again
stolen
equilibrium, separated loneliness
rare food for thought and the palate
(oh, the connection shrieks)
and the hungry ones call for more
(you're asking me How are you?)
And the sea's voice passes through my hearing
my flesh beats in my eyes' pulse
but I don't hear and I don't see
what it was
while I'm holding on to the bottom with a bone
muscles and fluidity increase
magnified and alone
in a mouthful I disappear
opened up
mother-of-pearl or a dry frost
I cannot tell them apart

Vera

Čejkovska

Born 1954 in Skopje. Studied science in Skopje and works at the Seismological Observatory there. Some volumes of poetry. Winner of a literary prize.

Memento

Melody
of dry memories

I call you
Nonsense
when in every movement
you seek themes
which have long been discovered

I call you
Madness
when in the impossible
you seek the possible
and vice versa

I close
all doors
all ears
I wrap myself
in deaf nights
and when in that muteness
you start whistling
I call you
Pitilessness

Impromptu

Do you ever
wish
to shatter the silence
to gather up all the chords on earth
and to compose the most beautiful symphony
just for yourself

Do you ever
wish
to bury blackness
to reach out for all colours
and to paint the most beautiful canvas
just for yourself

to crumble all space
to capture all time
to build an eternal castle
to hide away in it
'outlive everyone
just yourself

The well

Clear eye
of our need

We built you
and forgot you

But don't you forget
the days when
in your mirror
we saw ourselves
relaxed
smiling

In your depths
you shall hide our secrets

But for those
even today
who visit you
keep your
blue
and transparent
freshness

Clown

Each day
he whitens his face
into innocence
He reddens his cheeks
into shamefacedness
He raises his eyebrows
into astonishment
He saddens his eyes
into tears
He stretches his lips
into laughter
He inflates his nose
into anger
He extends his baldness
into experience
He enlarges his shoes
into certainty
He wears out his clothes
into tastelessness

Thus smartened up
in his
circus home
he makes us laugh
with the incongruity
between his inner motivations
and his outward movements.

Mosaic

From the coloured pieces
of our
shattered simplicity
we put together
our image

We press
frozen words
on immovable lips

and misty
secret eyes

Black strands
of our vagueness

Pale face
of our indecision

Footstep turned to stone

Still we seek ourselves

No matter how specific
that fragmented
expression in stone
it loses its meaning
under the pieces
of the absent sky.

The year of our Lord

Saint Clement inscribed an inspired Ego
upon the great phenomenal world
    I see the hagiographies, bright-hot dots.
    Under the vault of Ohrid's sky
    history is coolness, like
    an invisible oyster.
        And from the displayed lamb's brain in the freezer
        the supermarket knife
        extract the origin.

And when Clement opened the oyster, the pearls from him
were virtual skies above the empty square.

The box

The clock's metallic hands are licking
the numbers
and this algebra repeats itself
this algebra becomes a fugue
Into the jewelry box I replace the nibbled
pearls the broken bangles the torn necklaces.
The candles make the marble figurines dance
the curtains tremble:

The universe was once
an infinite void.

Slave Gorgo Dimoski

Born 1959 in a village near Ohrid.
Works as a schoolmaster. Several
volumes of poetry. Winner of two
prizes for young authors.

Every night I open my window

Every night
I open my window wide
for the bird
for my dear neighbour.

Then I go out.
It's easy for me in the sky
to collect
the fallen stars.

Every day I go through the same motions:
I return - And
at once
I open my window wide.

Revenge

The executioner arrives on the scene
and carefully raises his axe

that is his duty

      Out of turn
      leaning
      without beginning

through wellspring, future and light
flashes his sword - even then

in the dark dawn the miraculous dance
with the executioner is pure.

Consolation

After the play, after the scene, the same
undressing down to the blood

heavy breathing

Flinging of ornaments out of
the window   slithering
along one side of the sabre

Lowering the blinds, agreement
behind them   preparations

for the long marches, soaring
above the sharp rocks and also
racing in the morning

across the draw-well.

Rest

It's time to sit down
on the trodden butterflies
of our dream

To breathe within ourselves
to enter erect

A bird flies over us
a pensive billy-goat stands next to us
the wind strikes our heads
it certainly is a good day

in the upturned cup
above us.

We enter into ourselves down narrow pathways

Down narrow pathways we enter
into ourselves to the north
across the sea we enter south
each hour in early death
(unannounced and premature) into snow
which is slippery, we enter into mud
at a moment which will not change
the world and we'll blow through like a wind,
into the A and O, we enter within
the tongue, into what is otherwise
sticky-mouldy-sticky-misty,
which releases veins into the air, in this slight
link with power we enter into the madness
which smells
which smells of sperm.

Poem

I live but a single moment.
This moment I disappear and transform myself into a
sound-sheet
this moment is too long for my death and for my fragile life
but a single hour buried in the snow
in the horizon's echo, included in the flash.
In the steep slopes, in the wind-swept mane.
This day is too long for my fragile life
for the voice I raise. I live
this single moment, like the grass.
High as the sky one moment.
I have but a single moment and the last,
when I must wake and shout,
but one final moment when I shout,
when I begin and when I end,
when at the end I shout at the top of my voice,
I live but one single moment, one single hour,
this single day.

Aubade

Open your eye
like a soap bubble
to see yourself
flying
above the clouds
because while flying
you encourage the bird
in space
and the wind
to sweep along

Open also your other eye
to see yourself in the grass
melted in the dew
because by melting
you encourage the lather
smeared over your face
to hum a matutinal
tune
and a sigh
to warm you

And you look at yourself eye to eye
with two bubbles
rosy and quivering
because:

the bird drowns
in the air
and the wind
goes too far:
the lather is
smeared over the face
by the sigh which
warms you.

315,-

Other Yugoslavian Titles
from Forest Books

FOOTPRINTS OF THE WIND
by Mateja Matevski, translated by Ewald Osers.
Introduced by Robin Skelton 1988
0 948259 43 8   96 pages   £6.95 paper

LADY IN AN EMPTY DRESS
by Alexander Petrov, translated by Richard Burns 1990
0 948259 90 6   48 pages   £3.95 paper

I WEAR MY SHADOW INSIDE ME
by Duška Vrhovac, translated by Richard Burns
with Vera Radojević 1991
0 948259 91 4   48 pages   £3.95 paper

THROUGH THE NEEDLE'S EYE
by Jon Miloš, translated by Brenda Walker
with Jon Miloš 1990
0 948259 61 2   112 pages   £7.95 paper

THE TRAPPED STRAWBERRY
by Petru Cârdu, translated by Brenda Walker
with Dušica Marinkov 1990
Introduced by Daniel Weissbort
0 948259 83 3   96 pages   £6.95 paper

FOUR YUGOSLAVIAN PLAYS
The Black Hole by Goran Stefanovski
The Professional by by Dušan Kovačević
The Wall, the Lake by Dušan Jovanović
The Performance of Hamlet in Lower Ternwater
by Ivo Brešan
Edited by Brenda Walker
Introduced by Dragan Klaić 1992
0 948259 95 7   216 pages   £10.95 paper